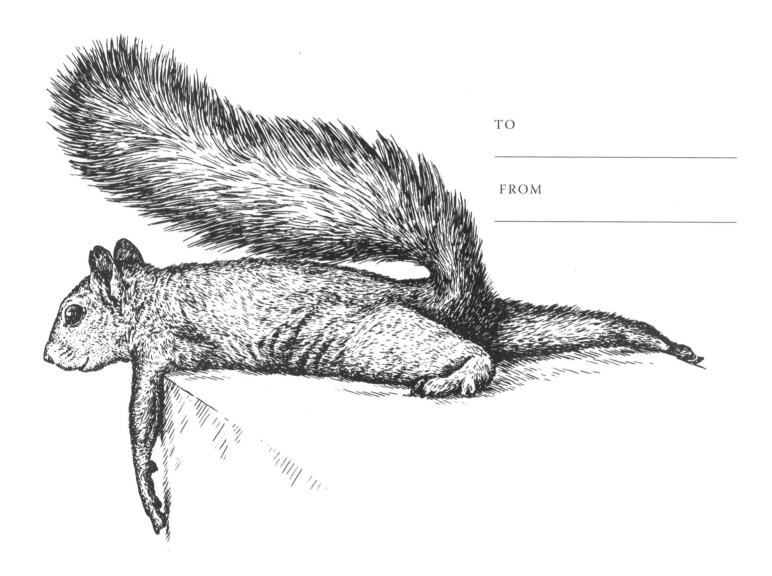

TO

_____

FROM

_____

KPT|PUBLISHING

CHANGING SEASONS

Published by KPT Publishing
Minneapolis, Minnesota 55406
www.KPTPublishing.com

ISBN 978-1-944833-03-9

Design and Development by
Koechel Peterson and Associates
Minneapolis, Minnesota

Images are courtesy of Shutterstock

First printing March 2017

10 9 8 7 6 5 4 3 2 1

Printed in the United States of America

The seasons are
what a symphony ought to be:
four perfect movements
in harmony with each other.

ARTHUR RUBENSTEIN

The best and most beautiful

things in the world

cannot be seen or even touched—

they must be felt with the heart.

HELEN KELLER

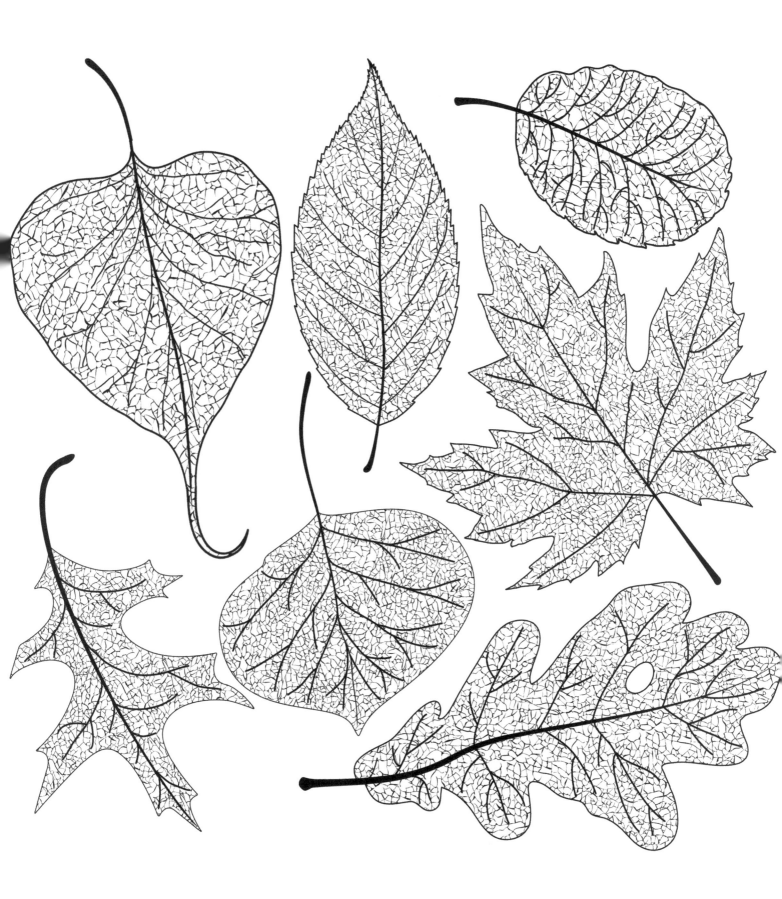

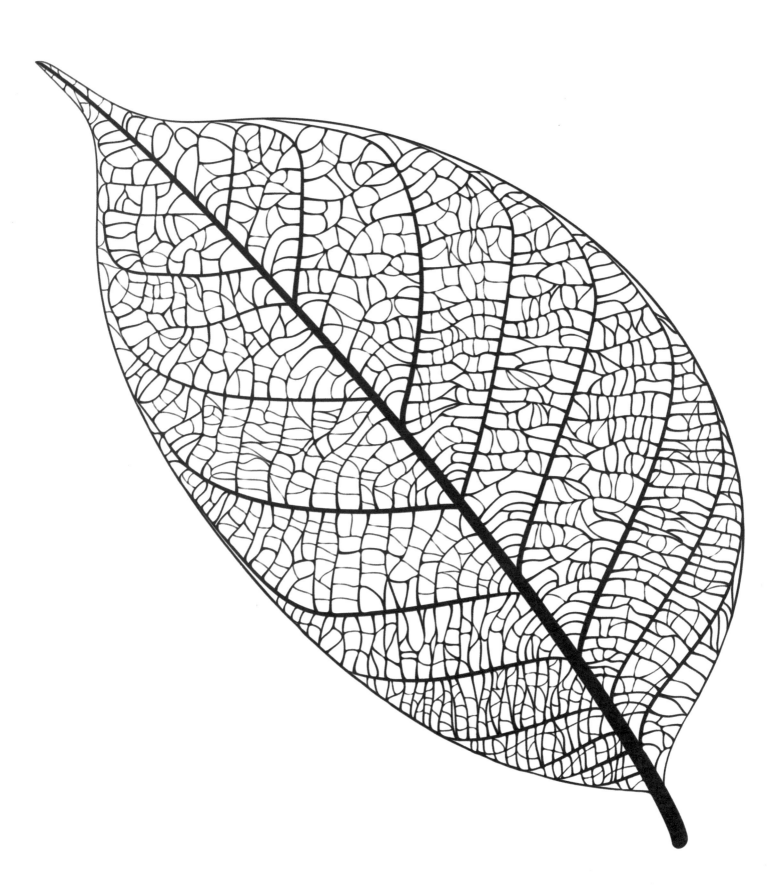

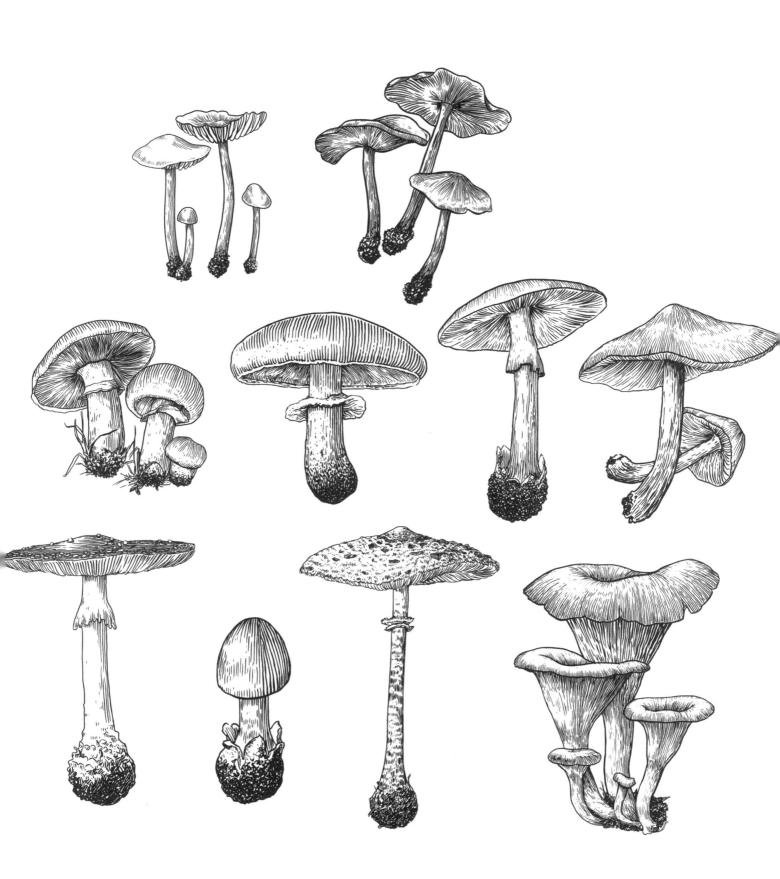

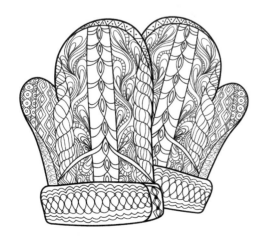

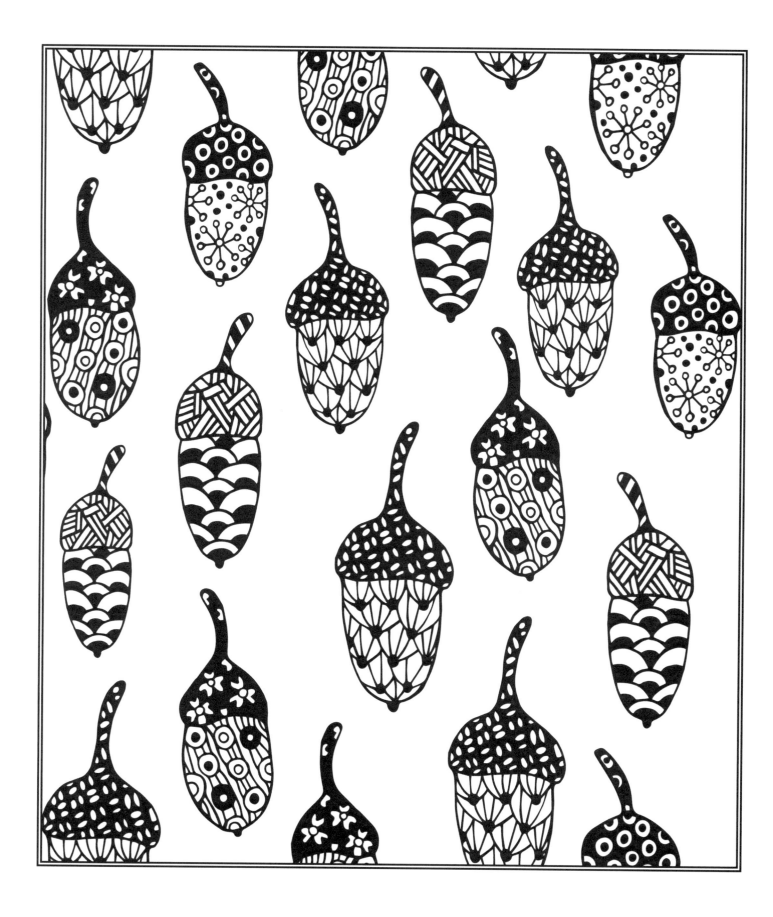

The flower

that smells the sweetest

is shy and lowly.

WILLIAM WORDSWORTH

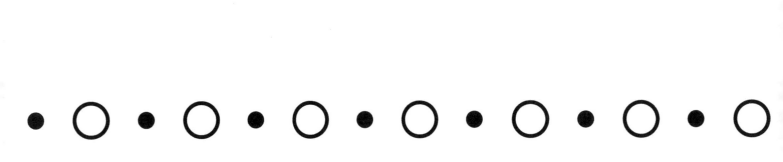

It is only the farmer

who faithfully plants seeds

in the Spring,

who reaps a harvest

in the Autumn.

B. C. FORBES

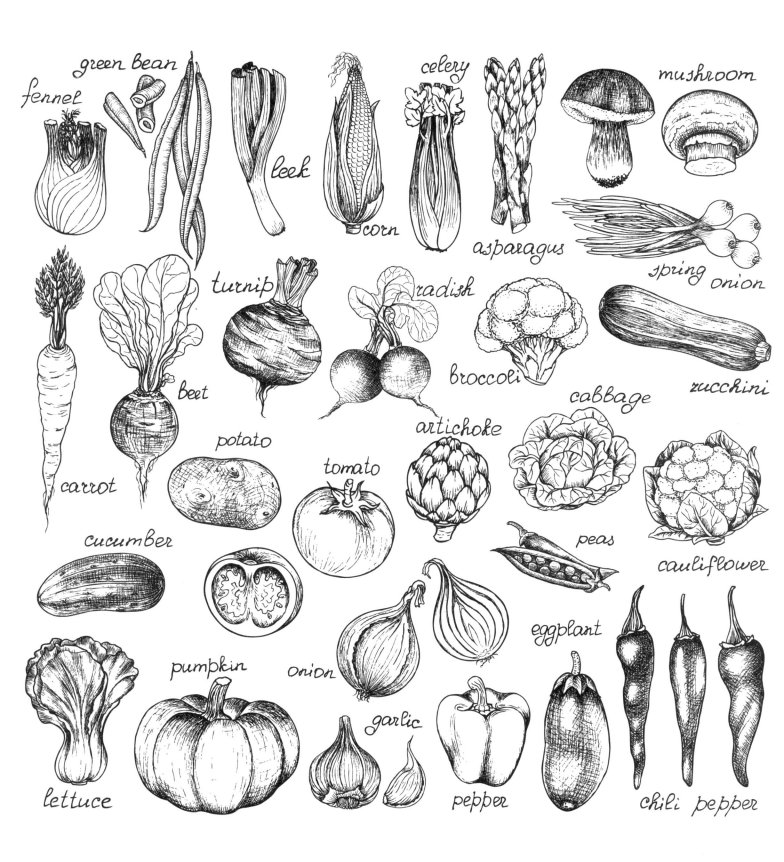

What is a weed?
*A plant whose virtues
have never been discovered.*

RALPH WALDO EMERSON

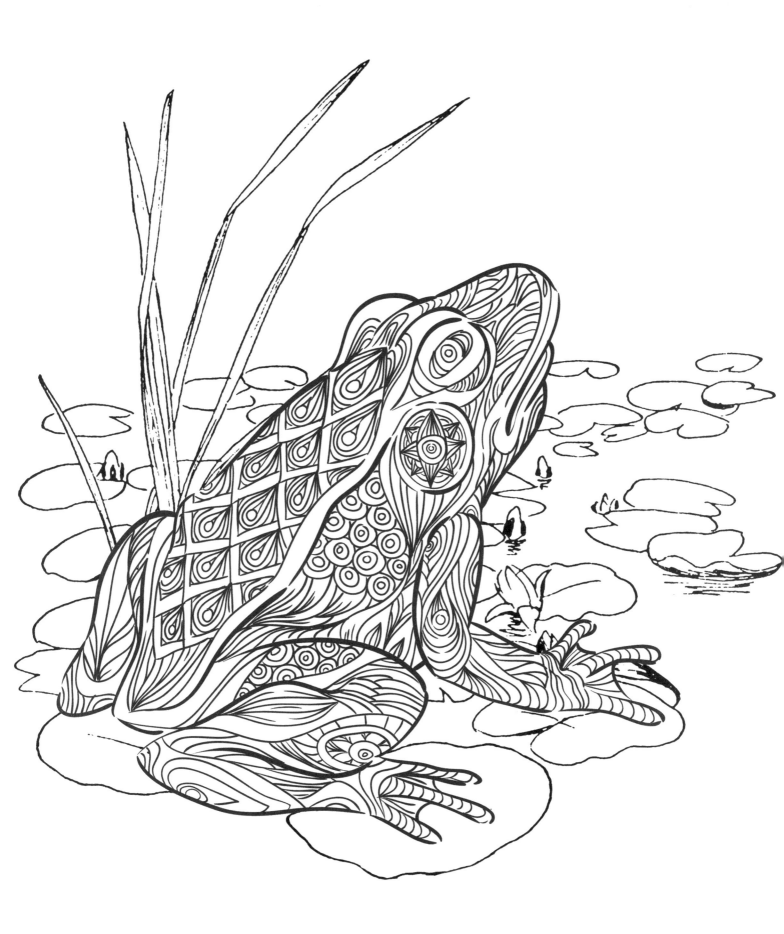